HOWLING
MOON BOOKS

ALSO AVAILABLE BY HOWLING MOON BOOKS

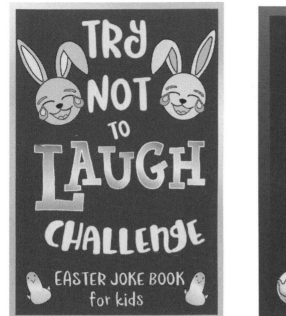

ROAD TRIP VACATION JOKES

IF YOU'RE LAUGHING, YOU'RE LOSING!
(BUT, YOU'RE HAVING LOTS OF FUN!)

Try Not to Laugh Challenge!

Rules:

Pick your team, or go one on one.

Sit across from each other & make eye contact.

Take turns reading jokes to each other.

You can make silly faces, funny sound effects, etc.

When your opponent laughs, you get a point!

First team to win 3 points, **Wins!**

If you're laughing, you're losing!
(But you are having lots of fun!)

What nationality are you
are in the bathroom?

European!

What is the most polite tower
in the world?

The Tower of Please. a!

What tower eats alot?

The I Full Tower!
(Eiffel)

What state abbreviation
would take the most
selfies?

ME! (Maine)

What abbreviated state is
a doctor?

MD! (Maryland)

What state abbreviation
is not feeling well?

IL! (Illinois)

What abbreviated state is
very friendly?

HI! (Hawaii)

Try Not to Laugh Challenge!

Rules:

Pick your team, or go one on one.

Sit across from each other & make eye contact.

Take turns reading jokes to each other.

You can make silly faces, funny sound effects, etc.

When your opponent laughs, you get a point!

First team to win 3 points, Wins!

If you're laughing, you're losing!
(But you are having lots of fun!)

What nationality are you if you
are in the bathroom?

European!

What is the most polite tower
in the world?

The Tower of Please-a!

What tower eats alot?

The I Full Tower!
(Eiffel)

What state abbreviation is just
like mom and dad?

MA & PA!
(Massachusetts) & (Pennsylvania)

What abbreviated state is just
fine with everything?

OK! (Oklahoma)

What state is a number?

Ten-nessee

What state recycles the most?

Kans-as!

What is Noah's
favorite state?

Ark-ansas!

What is a waffle's favorite
vacation beach?

Sandy Eggo!

Did the skunk family have
a good vacation?

No, it stunk!

Did the owl family have
a nice vacation?

Yes, it was a hoot!

What is a dog's favorite place
to visit in Rome, Italy?

Collie-see-um!
(Colosseum)

Why couldn't the spy do his job?

Because he had spy-arrhea!

What kind of meat do rocket
scientists put in their sandwich?

Launch meat!

Why did the plane get sent
to it's room?

Bad altitude!

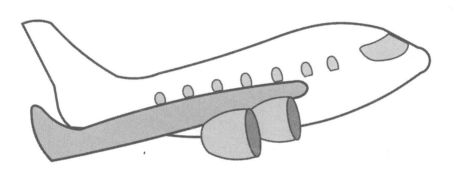

What kind of dogs like to fly?

Airedales

Who lives in the water and
helps old fish?

A boy trout!

What do you call a tiger with
no teeth?

A tiger lily!

What is gray, has a long, pointy
tooth and a trunk?

A narwhal going on vacation!

What is tan, has a long pointy
tooth, and a trunk?

A narwhal coming back
from vacation!

What is red, has a long, pointy
tooth, and a trunk?

A sunburned narwhal coming
back from vacation!

Why is H the most popular letter
in the alphabet?

Because every holiday starts
with it!

Where do horses go on vacation?

Neigh-braska and Neigh-vada!

What do pigs like to do
in the summer?

Go on pig-nics!

Why was the watch tense?

Because he was all wound up!

When can't you vacation
on the moon?

When it is full!

What do you call a girl
at the beach?

Sandy!

Why did the moon burp?

It was full!

How do you greet a toad?

Warts new?

Why doesn't anyone want to vacation on the planets in our solar system?

Because they don't have any atmosphere!

What happens when sheep drive cars?

They make ewe turns!

What do you get when you cross
a toad with a dog?

A croaker spaniel!

What state do ducks like to go
on vacation?

Duck-ota!

What do you call a cow droid?

Moo2D2!

What is a dog's favorite vegetable?

Arf-ichokes!

Why did the moose want to come inside the house?

Because there were too many moose-quitos outside!

What do frogs like to drink on
a hot summer day?

Croak-a-cola!

What do bees say in the summer?

It's swarm out here!

What are butterflies afraid of?

The mam-moth!

What state has a lot of cats
and dogs?

Petsylvania!

Why are dogs like cell phones?

Because they have collar IDs!

What did the dinosaur say after he hiked up the mountain?

I'm so-asaurus!

What kind of beans glow at night?

Moon beans!

How do dogs travel?

On a mutt-a-cycle!

Where do horses go on their honeymoon?

Niagara Stalls!

Who travels the most?

Romans!

Why are forests like computers?

They both have bugs!

Knock, knock.
Who's there?
Jethro.
Jethro who?

Jethro the boat and
stop talking!

Knock, knock.
Who's there?
Candy.
Candy who?

Candy please stop talking
and row the boat!

Knock, knock.
Who's there?
Romeo.
Romeo who?

Just Romeo across the lake!

Knock, knock.
Who's there?
Madrid.
Madrid who?

Madrid you pack my
bathing suit?
(Mom did)

Knock, knock.
Who's there?
Paris.
Paris who?

Mom, did you pack me a
Paris pants?

Knock, knock.
Who's there?
Everest.
Everest who?

Do you Everest from hiking?

Knock, knock.
Who's there?
Italy.
Italy who?

Italy so much fun when
vacation starts!

Knock, knock.
Who's there?
Europe.
Europe who?

Are Europe for a swim
in the ocean?

Knock, knock.
Who's there?
Japan.
Japan who?

Where is Japan for
making pancakes?

Knock, knock.
Who's there?
Spain.
Spain who?

Spain when sand sticks to
everything when you get wet
at the beach!

Knock, knock.
Who's there?
Quebec.
Quebec who?

Quebec to the hotel room and
get my sunglasses!

Knock, knock.
Who's there?
Germany.
Germany who?

Turn off your phone, you are
getting Germany texts!

Knock, knock.
Who's there?
India.
India who?

Let's all get India car now
for our road trip!

Knock, knock.
Who's there?
Utah.
Utah who?

Utah-ing to your friend again,
turn off that cell phone!

Knock, knock.
Who's there?
Sicily.
Sicily who?

Let's try not to get too Sicily
at the fancy restaurant!

Knock, knock.
Who's there?
Asia.
Asia who?

Asia suitcase in the car yet?

Knock, knock.
Who's there?
Israel.
Israel who?

Israel good to finally be
on vacation!

How do fireflies start a race?

Ready, set, glow!

What do you call a boy with
a shovel?

Doug!

What do golfers have with their
scrambled eggs?

Toast with putter on it!

What can you pick in a flower
garden that you can't
put in a vase?

A guitar!

What do you call a space ship that
is sorry for everything?

Apollo G!

What is a sloth's favorite
historical figure?

Nap-oleon!

What kind of tea do aliens drink?

Gravi-tea!

What kind of bath can you
take without water?

A sun bath!

What did the boy say when
the alien left Earth?

E.T. come, E.T. go!

Why do astronauts make good
friends?

They are all down to earth!

What did the family say to the Statue of Liberty?

Stay in torch!

How does grandma mail her meatballs?

Through the pasta office!

What is a dog's favorite baseball team?

New York Mutts!

Why didn't the boy want to
use toothpaste?

Because none of his teeth
were loose!

What kind of game do insects
like to play?

Fris-bee!

What is a lion's favorite state?

Maine!

Where do Russians get
their milk?

Mos-cows!

What do you call an angry
monkey?

Furious George!

What state has the most colors?

Color-ado!

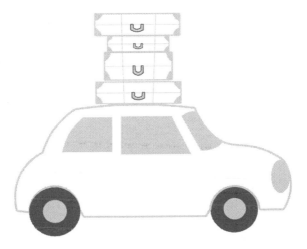

What state only has one
movie star in it?

The Lone Star State!

What kind of people travel
really fast?

Russians!

What kind of car tells
lots of jokes?

Jolkswagon!

What do you say when your
hog runs away?

Hoggone!

What day do you drink the
most water?

Thirst-day!

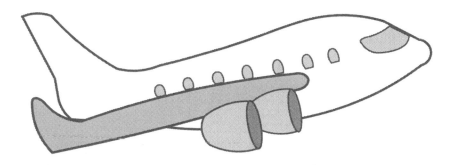

What do passengers on a plane
and football players have
in common?

They both want good
touchdowns!

Why shouldn't you fart in an
Apple store?

Because there are no windows!

What snack do dogs like to eat
when they watch movies?

A bowl of pupcorn and 7-pup!

What did the astronaut say
when he was asked about
the black hole?

No comet!

What is the smartest spy
in the world?

Albert Spyingstein!

Who makes the fastest
underwear?

Fruit of the zoom!

How do you send a message
to your dad?

Insta-man!

Why don't aliens like to visit
our planet?

It only has a one star rating!

What shouldn't you eat
for breakfast if you don't
want to fart?

Tootmeal!

Where were the first
french fries cooked?

In Greece!

What did the alien bird say
to the Earth bird?

Take me to your feeder!

I would like to go to Sweden one day.

Wooden shoe?

Why is sign language so cool?

Because it's handy!

What kind of tea do hockey players drink?

Penal-tea!

What do you call a computer superhero?

A screen saver!

Why should you never touch an alien frog?

Star warts!

What country in Europe takes care of Hungary?

Turkey!

What do you call a girl in the
middle of a tennis court?

Annette!

What kind of candy do you eat
on the playground?

Recess pieces!

What do you call a slow skier?

A slopepoke!

What kind of dance parties do
skiers go to?

Snowballs!

Where does a skier keep
his money?

In the snow bank!

What is a fish's favorite musical instrument?

The bass guitar!

Where does a fish get his hair cut?

The bobber shop!

What fish is not allowed in a library?

The big-mouthed bass!

Why did the vegetarians skip the weekend swimming competition?

They don't like meets!

What kind of dive is the military good at?

Cannon balls!

What is a whale's favorite swim stroke?

The blubber-fly!

What day of the week do people fart the most?

Tootsday!

What is a boxer's favorite drink?

Fruit punch!

Why can't you ever get any computer work out of a cat?

Because they are always playing with the mouse!

Why are bank tellers good
at surfing?

Because they know how
to balance!

What kind of tree can you
find on the beach?

Crab apple tree!

Why were the kids mad about
the new pirate movie?

Because it was rated ARRRR,
so they couldn't go!

Why does the cheerleader put extra salt on her food?

So she could do summer salts!

Where do ants go on vacation?

Frants!

Where do eggs go on vacation?

New Yolk City!

Where do you go to dance
in California?

San Frandisco!

What is a unicorn's favorite
musical instrument?

The uni-cordion!

What insect is a computer geek?

Spiders, because they are
always on the web!

What do you call a cat that likes
to eat refried beans?

Puss n' Toots!

What kind of party do shellfish
go to?

A clambake!

What does a unicorn eat
for breakfast?

Only cereal that's magically
delicious!

How do unicorns buy things?

With corn "bread"!

What do you call a city without little apples?

Mini-apple-less!

What is a unicorn's favorite cereal?

Unicornflakes!

How do you get a surfer
to school on time?

Tell him there are no waves!

What is an easy way to make
music?

Buy a headband!

Why do bad singers never get
in trouble?

Because they never hit the notes!

What kind of songs do you sing
in a car?

Cartoons!

Knock, knock.
Who's there?
Maida.
Maida who?

Maida force be with you!

What do cars do at parties?

Brake dance!

Where does Santa like to go
on vacation?

Jolly-wood!

Why do cows go to France?

To see the Moo-na Lisa!

What do dogs eat for
breakfast?

Wooffles!

When is a dog's favorite time to
go to the bathroom?

Two turdy!

Where do dogs like to go
on vacation?

Collie-wood!

Knock, knock.
Who's there?
Al.
Al who?

Al be on vacation
all summer!

Knock, knock.
Who's there?
Jane.
Jane who?

Jane into a bathing suit
so we can go swimming!

Knock, knock.
Who's there?
Ben.
Ben who?

Ben on any good
road trips lately?

Knock, knock.
Who's there?
Justin.
Justin who?

You are Justin time for
another vacation joke!

Knock, knock.
Who's there?
Wayne.
Wayne who?

Wayne, Wayne, go away.
I'm on my vacation!

Knock, knock.
Who's there?
Ketchup.
Ketchup who?

I'll ketchup with you later if
you go to the beach!

What do you get when you cross
a moose with an insect?

Moose-quito!

What do you get when you cross
a goat and a cow?

Half and Half!

Why did the cell phone share his
food with the other cell phone?

Because he had too much
to tweet!

What do cows wear in Hawaii?

Moo Moos!

What show do cows
like to watch?

Let's milk a deal!

What do you call a crab
that talks too much?

A gabby crabby!

What do you call a DVD
for kids?

A kid vid!

What do you call a very
friendly bug?

A hug bug!

What do you call a shore
full of clams?

Clam jam!

Why did the ear of corn start
turning into popcorn
on the beach?

He forgot to wear his sunscreen!

How do trees get on the internet?

They log in!

What did the parrot say when
his computer was attacked?

Poly doesn't want a hacker!

Where do pigs stay if they go
to Alaska for vacation?

Pig-loos!

Why can't you give kids ravioli
late at night?

Because it's pasta
their bedtime!

Where do roosters go out to eat?

Roostaurants!

Where do ducks go on vacation?

Ken-ducky!

Where do angry skiers
go on vacation?

Cross-country trips!

What is the difference between
a boy in a superhero costume
riding a tricycle and
a boy in a dinosaur costume
riding a bicycle ?

Attire!

Where do song birds go
on vacation?

Canary Islands!

What do you call a dog droid?

Arf2D2!

Why did the dog cross the road?

To pant on the other side!

What kind of dog would make
a good breakfast?

A beagle with cream cheese!

Why did the dog get detention
at obedience school?

He forgot to wear his
Cats Stink t-shirt!

What state has the most cows?

Moo Jersey!

What is a sloth's
favorite mountain?

Mount Ever-rest!

Why should you bring your own
food on a small plane?

Because the food is
a little plane!

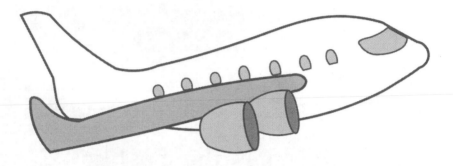

What state has the
most astronauts?

Moon-tana!

Why did the librarian get kicked
off the plane?

It was overbooked!

Where do computers stay when
they go camping?

Blog cabins!

What pets do computers try
to stay away from?

Spamsters!

How do you wake up
a sleep walker?

Put bubble wrap on the floor!

Where do aliens go boating?

In the galax-seas!

What did the alien mom
say to her son after he
wondered off while they
were on vacation on Earth?

Where on Earth have you been!

Where is the cinnamon man from?

Outer spice!

What do you say to a boy computer
when he does a good job?

Data boy!

Why do chickens like to visit
New York City?

Because they like to go to the
Henspire State Building!

What did the cell phone say
to the land line?

Hi grandma!

What kind of mail do you wish
you had on a hot day?

Fan mail!

What kind of dog do you wish
you had on a hot day?

Pupsicle!

Where do sharks go
on vacation?

Finland!

What does seaweed say when
it is stuck on the bottom
of a boat?

Kelp! Kelp!

What do you call a
sad girl scout?

A girl pout!

How do you call someone
if you are in Africa?

Drop them a lion!

What country is like a coin?

Guinea!

What country is very angry?

Ireland!

What country is very sad?

Wales!

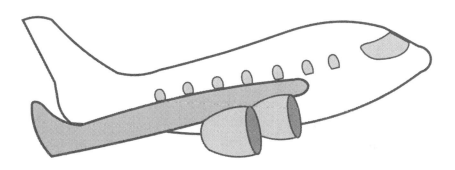

What country is popular on
Thanksgiving?

Turkey!

What country is always looking for something to eat?

Hungary!

What country do you need on the dinner table?

China!

What is a skater's favorite country?

Iceland!

What is a chef's favorite country?

Greece!

Why is England the wettest
country?

Because the Queen has
reigned there for years!

Who would dare sit in front of the
Queen of England
with his hat on?

Her chauffeur!

What do you call an Italian
fidget spinner?

A pizza slicer!

Where do sausage and mushrooms
go on vacation?

The leaning
Tower of Pizza!

Knock, knock.
Who's there?
Tijuana.
Tijuana who?

Tijuana bring some games
on vacation?

Knock, knock.
Who's there?
Venice.
Venice who?

Venice our family leaving
for vacation?

Knock, knock.
Who's there?
China.
China who?

I'm China to get ready
for vacation!

Knock, knock.
Who's there?
Bayou.
Bayou who?

I'll Bayou all ice cream
when we get to the beach!

What do you call a Roman
with a cold?

Julius Sneezer!

What do you call a Roman who
annoys girls?

Julius Teaser!

How do cats and dogs start
a race?

Ready Pet Go!

What do you call a little hippo?

Hippo-tot-amus!

What color is a burp?

Burple!

What is the best day to go
to the beach?

Sun-day!

What kind of music scares
hot air balloons?

Pop music!

What sound does a nut make
when it sneezes?

Cashew!

Knock, knock.
Who's there?
Alpaca.
Alpaca who?

Alpaca the trunk, you
pack the suitcase!

Knock, knock.
Who's there?
Anita.
Anita who?

Anita vacation right
now!

Knock, knock.
Who's there?
Poop.
Poop who?

LOL!
Made you say
Poo Poo!

Knock, knock.
Who's there?
Weirdo.
Weirdo who?

Weirdo you want
to go on vacation?

Knock, knock.
Who's there?
Yacht.
Yacht who?

Yachts up Doc?

Knock, knock.
Who's there?
Jamaica.
Jamaica who?

Jamaica me crazy with all
the jokes we have to hear
on vacation!

Where do ants like to go
on a beach vacation?

Ant-lantic City!

What girls name has a nice
ring to it?

Belle!

What is a pirate's
favorite vegetable?

Arrrr-tichokes!

What pirate likes to tell
lots of jokes?

Captain Kidd!

Why does it take pirates so long
to learn the alphabet?

Because they spend all
their time at C!

What do aliens drink
on the moon?

Craterade!

What does it mean if astronauts
find a cow skeleton on the moon?

Maybe she didn't make it
over the moon!

Why don't skeletons go on vacation?

Because they have nobody
to go with!

Why did the mummy
go on vacation?

He needed to unwind!

What does a monster drink
on vacation?

Ghoul-aid!

Where do ghosts like to
go fishing?

Lake Eerie!

How do ghouls like to travel?

Fright trains!

Where do bees go
on vacation?

Stingapore!

What grows on trees and
is really strong?

Hercu-leaves!

Why did the flea bring
salsa and chips to the party?

Because it was a flea-esta!

What did one mosquito say
to the other mosquito?

Want to go out for a bite?

How do garden gnomes travel?

Mobile gnomes!

How do cows travel?

On moo-torcycles!

What is a cow's favorite
state to go on vacation?

Cow-lifornia!

What is a cow's favorite
country to go on vacation?

Moo Zealand!

Where do hamsters go
on vacation?

Hampsterdam!

What did the kids say when
mom couldn't make pancakes?

How waffle!

What did the mom cupcake
say to the kid cupcake?

You bake me crazy!

How do billboards talk?

Sign language!

What country is always
getting bigger?

Ireland, because it's capital
is Dublin!

What kind of people never
go on vacation?

Calendar makers, because
they can't take days off!

If spaghetti made a motion picture,
what would it be called?

Mission Im-pasta-ble!

What letter can travel
the farthest?

The letter D, it goes to the
end of the world!

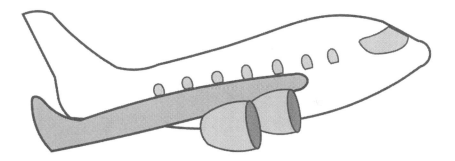

What do you eat for lunch
on the beach?

Sand-wiches!

Why shouldn't you iron your
four leaf clover?

You don't want to
press your luck!

Why shouldn't you crush
your soda cans?

Because it's soda pressing!

What did the camper say when
he was hit by lightning?

Time to glow now!

What do computer geeks eat
at a party?

A byte of everything!

Why didn't the camper want to
sleep on the top bunk?

He didn't want to oversleep!

How do pimples send messages?

Zwitter!

Why is it OK to buy a chimp
at the pet store?

Because they have a
monkey back guarantee!

Why did the egg cross the road?

It thought it would be
egg-citing!

Where did the cheese want
to go on vacation?

To the Swiss Alps!

Knock, knock.
Who's there?
Alaska.
Alaska who?

Alaska mom where we are
going for vacation this year!

Knock, knock.
Who's there?
Lily.
Lily who?

Lily be leaving soon
for vacation?

Knock, knock.
Who's there?
Wyatt.
Wyatt who?

Wyatt taking so long to
leave for vacation?

Knock, knock.
Who's there?
Lorraine.
Lorraine who?

Lorraine is falling,
pack your umbrellas!

Knock, knock.
Who's there?
August.
August who?

That August of wind
was cold!

Knock, knock.
Who's there?
Ooze.
Ooze who?

Ooze in charge of planning
our vacation?

Knock, knock.
Who's there?
Icing.
Icing who?

Icing in the shower on
vacation every morning!

Knock, knock.
Who's there?
Aaron.
Aaron who?

The Aaron this cabin
has a dusty smell!

Knock, knock.
Who's there?
Ammonia.
Ammonia who?

Ammonia one person, I can't
pack the car by myself!

Knock, knock.
Who's there?
Dishes.
Dishes who?

Dishes the first day of
summer vacation!

Knock, knock.
Who's there?
Freddy.
Freddy who?

Freddy or not vacation,
here we come!

Knock, knock.
Who's there?
Goat.
Goat who?

Goat to go now,
camp starts this morning!

Knock, knock.
Who's there?
Giddy up.
Giddy up who?

Giddy up so we can go to
the beach!

Knock, knock.
Who's there?
Hugo.
Hugo who?

Will Hugo swimming with me
today?

Knock, knock.
Who's there?
Harvey.
Harvey who?

Harvey going canoeing
today?

What do you call a gnome with blue hair?

Mrs. Gnomer Simpson!

Why do you want alpacas to go camping with you?

Because they always say alpaca the tents for you!

What song do hornets like to sing?

I'm stinging in the rain!

What kind of gum do bees chew?

Bumble gum!

What do bees pack for the beach?

Their bee-kinis!

What do humming birds eat
at picnics?

Hum-burgers

What do you call a person who can't flip pancakes?

A flip flop!

Knock, knock.
Who's there?
Canoe.
Canoe who?

Canoe find someone who knows how to flip pancakes!

Where do sheep go on vacation?

The Baaa-hamas!

What do you call a sheep
covered in chocolate?

A candy baa!

Knock, knock.
Who's there?
Havana.
Havana who?

We're Havana a great time
on vacation!

Knock, knock.
Who's there?
Iran.
Iran who?

Iran around all day getting us
ready for vacation!

What should you give a
carsick kid?

A bus ticket!

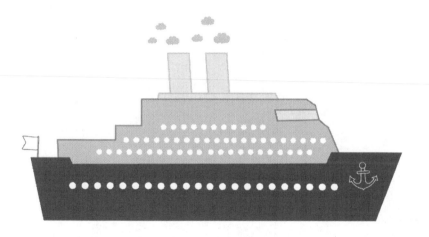

Why should a unicorn carry
a whistle?

Because they're horns don't work!

What happens when you
unplug a fan?

It loses it's cool!

What did the blog say to
the ice cream cone?

What's the scoop?

What do you call a snowman on spring break?

A puddle!

What do you call a Frenchman wearing beach sandals?

Phillipe Phloppe!

Why did the car have a
stomach ache?

Too much gas!

What do you get when you eat
refried beans and onions?

Tear gas!

What is Ben Franklin's favorite
ice cream flavor?

Shock-olate!

What did the angry sushi roll say?

No more mister rice guy!

Why did the math student go
to the beach?

He wanted to be a tan gent!

What do you call a
Jamaican cop?

A police-mon!

What are Jamaicans afraid of?

The boogie-mon!

How do Jamaicans send messages?

Insta-mon!

What type of donuts do you
find in a Jamaican bakery?

Cinna-mon!

Why didn't the Unicorn pillow
want a donut?

Because it was stuffed!

What do you find in a
clean nose?

Fingerprints!

Why did the girl give up
tap dancing?

Because she kept falling
in the sink!

How do you plant
mushrooms in the garden?

Far apart, they need as
mushroom as possible!

What is an astronaut's favorite key
on the computer?

The space bar!

Why did the teacher give the
firefly a bathroom pass?

Because when you gotta glow,
you gotta glow!

What is a coffee lover's favorite song?

Latte Be!

How are coffee beans like kids?

They are always getting grounded!

What kind of dog can open
a door?

A Corg-key!

How can you tell that you have
seen the Milky Way?

It's passed your eyes!

Why can't you keep the alphabet together in the garden?

Because the B will take off for the flowers!

What do you call someone who can't stay on a diet?

A desserter!

What is a kid's idea of a balanced diet?

A cupcake in each hand!

How do Superheros dream?

Mightmares!

How do giraffe's dream?

Heightmares!

Where do ducks go on vacation?

Alba-quacky, New Mexico!

Where do birds like to go on vacation?

Fowl-adelphia!

Where did the dentist go
on vacation?

The mouth of the Mississippi!

Where did the plumber go
on vacation?

Flushing, New York!

Where did the nurse go
on vacation?

Ill-inois!

Where did the fortune teller go
on vacation?

Palm Beach!

Where do coyotes go
on vacation?

Howl-iday Inn!

What do you need when
you are being attacked
by mosquitoes?

The swat team!

What can you find in the
little mermaid's office?

Shell phone and clamputer!

If a shark is chasing you, what can you throw at it?

Jawbreakers!

Who won the zombie war?

No one, it was dead even!

Where does a zombie live?

On a dead end street!

What monster is the best dancer?

The boogie man!

What is a ghost's favorite fruit?

A boo-nana!

What kind of pants do
ghosts wear?

Boo-jeans!

What do you call a smart unicorn?

An "A" corn!

What kind of food does Ken like
to bring to the beach?

Barbie-Q-chicken!

Knock, knock.
Who's there?
Gladys.
Gladys who?

Aren't you Gladys summer
vacation!

Knock, knock.
Who's there?
Rob.
Rob who?

Rob some sunscreen on my back!

Knock, knock.
Who's there?
Norway.
Norway who?

There is Norway I want
vacation to end!

Knock, knock.
Who's there?
Rhino.
Rhino who?

Rhino, you don't want
vacation to end!

Knock, knock.
Who's there?
Badger
Badger who?

Too badger vacation is over now!

Knock, knock.
Who's there?
Sarah.
Sarah who?

Sarah another vacation after
this one?

HOWLING
MOON BOOKS

Made in the USA
Columbia, SC
13 April 2019